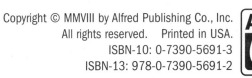

MEGAHITS of 2008

13 Pop, Rock, Country and Dance Music Chartbusters

ARRANGED BY JERRY RAY

Contents

Copyright © MMVIII by Alfred Publishing Co., Inc.
All rights reserved.   Printed in USA.
ISBN-10: 0-7390-5691-3
ISBN-13: 978-0-7390-5691-2

All-American Girl

Words and Music by
Carrie Underwood, Kellie Lovelace and Ashley Gorley
Arranged by Jerry Ray

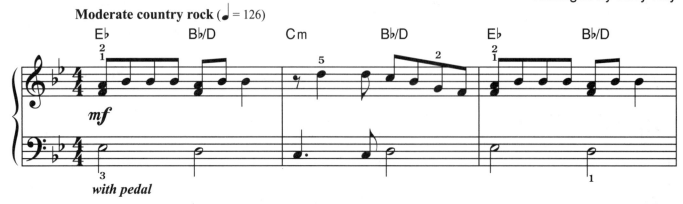

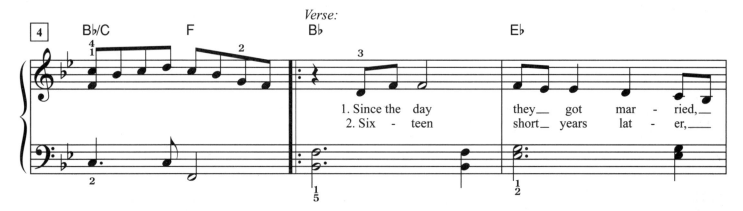

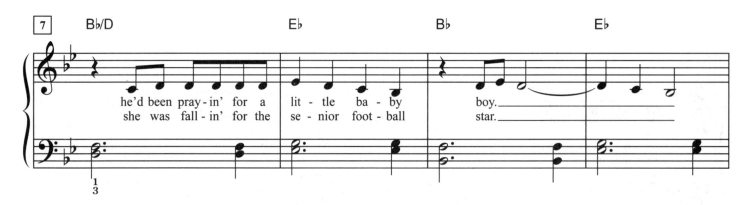

Because of You

Words and Music by
Kelly Clarkson, Ben Moody and David Hodges
Arranged by Jerry Ray

Celebrate Me Home

Lyrics by Kenny Loggins
Music by Kenny Loggins and Bob James
Arranged by Jerry Ray

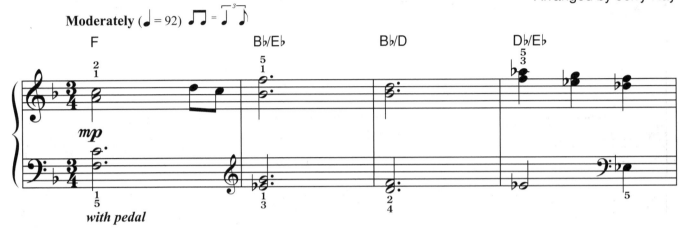

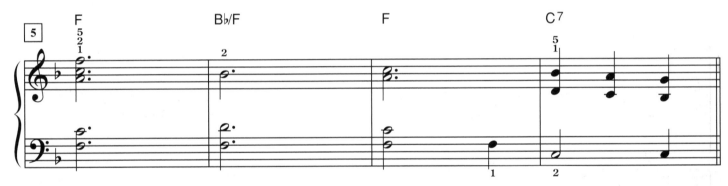

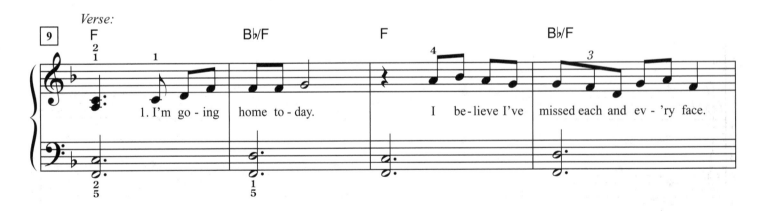

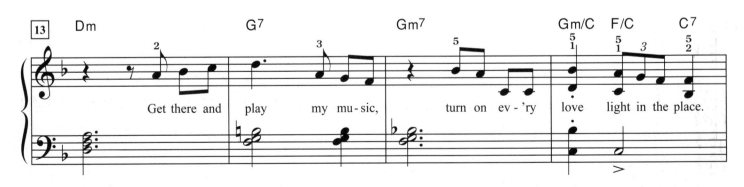

14

Don't Stop the Music

Words and Music by
Michael Jackson, Mikkel Storleer Eriksen,
Tor Erik Hermansen and Frankie Storm
Arranged by Jerry Ray

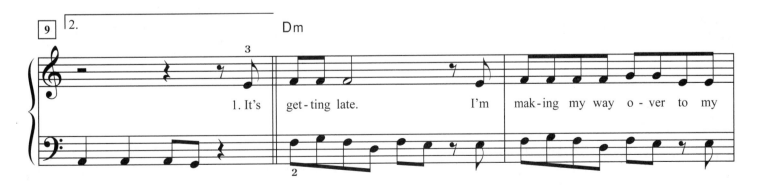

* The left hand may be played one octave lower throughout.

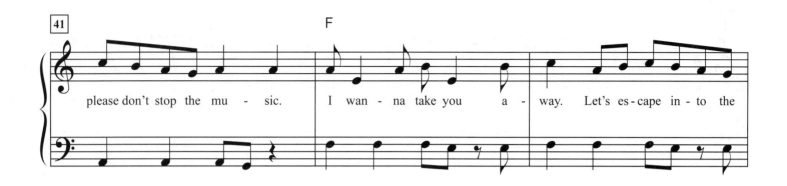

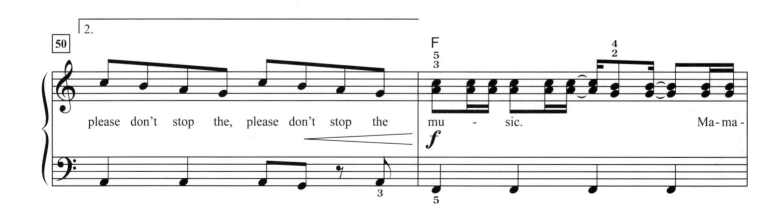

se ma-ma-sa ma-ma-coo-sa.___ Ma-ma- se ma-ma-sa ma-ma - coo - sa,___ ma-ma-

se ma-ma-sa ma-ma-coo-sa.___ Ma-ma- se ma-ma-sa ma-ma - coo - sa,___ ma-ma-

se ma-ma-sa ma-ma-coo-sa.___ Ma-ma- se ma-ma-sa ma-ma - coo - sa,___ ma-ma-

se ma-ma-sa ma-ma-coo - sa.___ Please don't stop the mu - sic.

Hey There Delilah

Words and Music by Tom Higgenson
Arranged by Jerry Ray

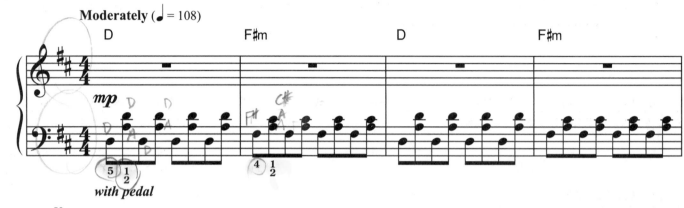

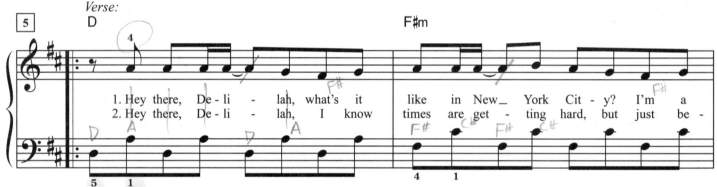

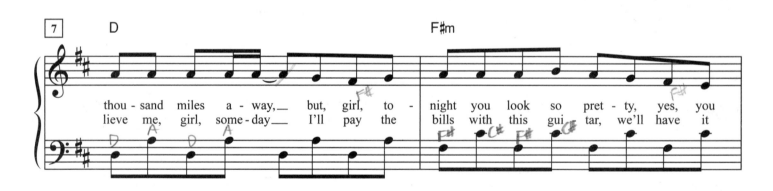

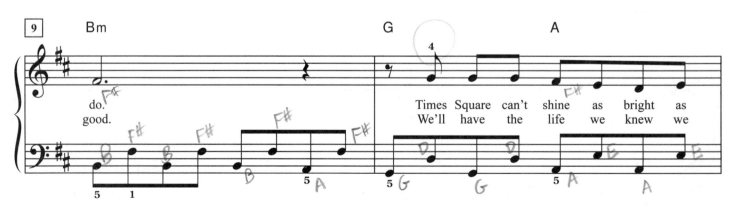

Everything

Words and Music by
Michael Bublé, Alan Chang and Amy Foster-Gilles
Arranged by Jerry Ray

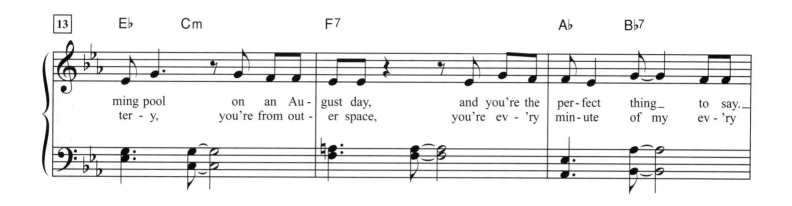

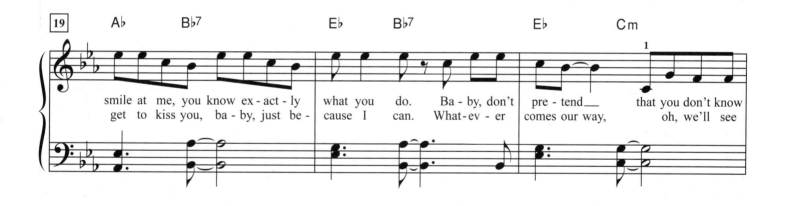

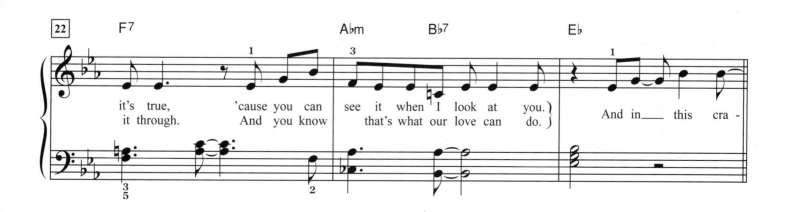

I Kissed a Girl

Words and Music by
Katy Perry, Lukasz Gottwald,
Max Martin and Cathy Dennis
Arranged by Jerry Ray

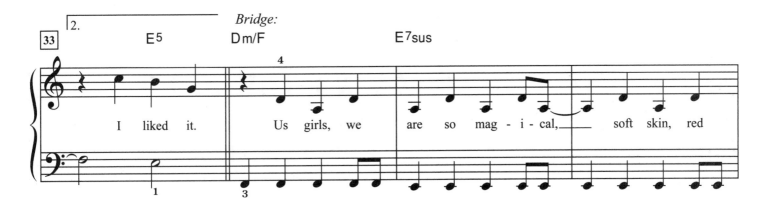

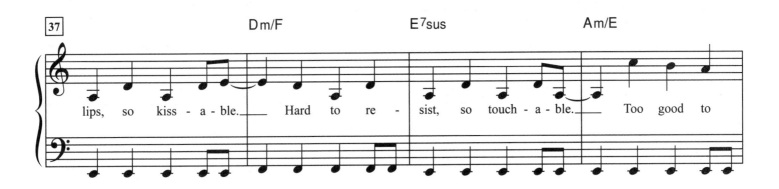

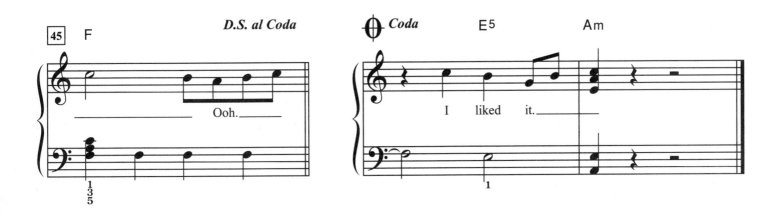

I'll Stand by You

Words and Music by
Billy Steinberg, Chrissie Hynde and Tom Kelly
Arranged by Jerry Ray

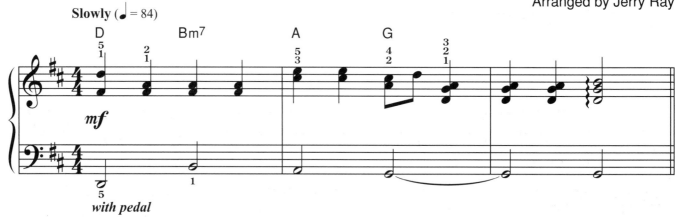

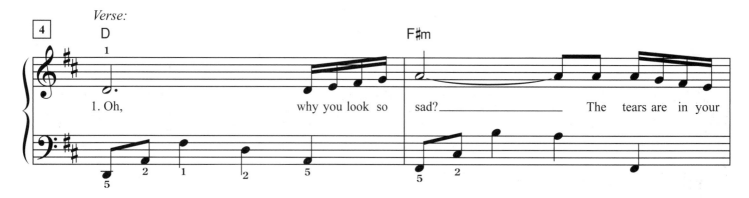

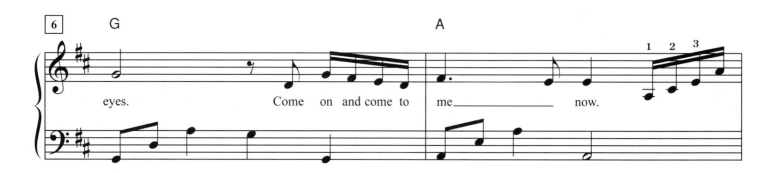

Lost

Words and Music by
Michael Bublé, Alan Chang and Jann Arden
Arranged by Jerry Ray

New Soul

Words and Music by
Yael Naim and David Donatien
Arranged by Jerry Ray

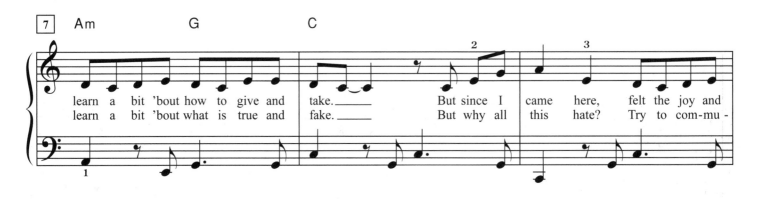

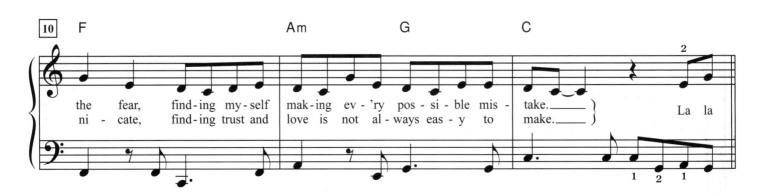

Rockstar

Lyrics by Chad Kroeger
Music by Nickelback
Arranged by Jerry Ray

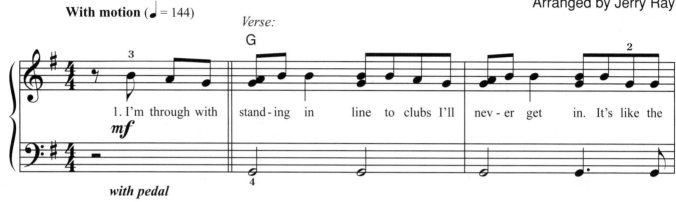

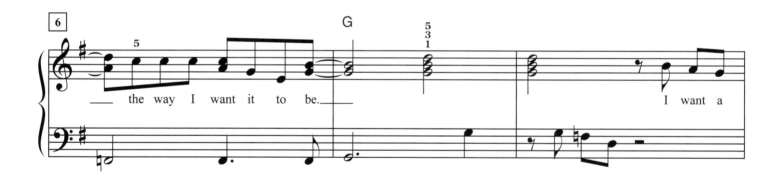

49

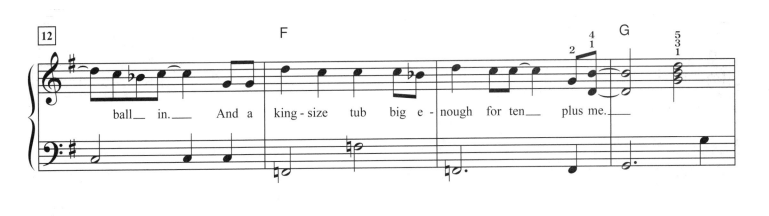

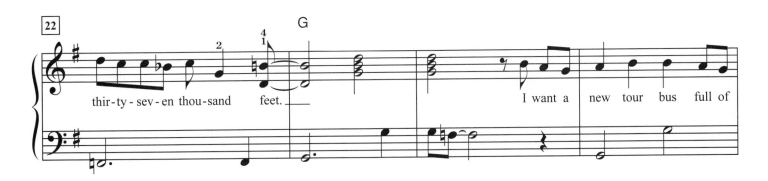

be - tween Cher and James Dean is fine for me.

I'm gon - na trade this life for for - tune and fame, I'd e - ven

Chorus:

cut my hair and change my name. 'Cause we all just wan - na be

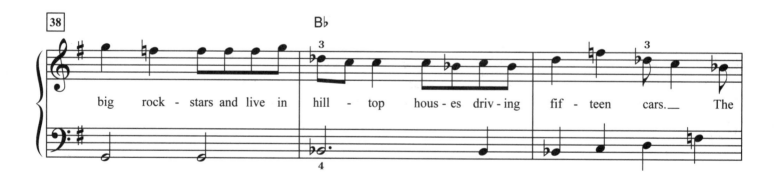

big rock - stars and live in hill - top hous - es driv - ing fif - teen cars. The

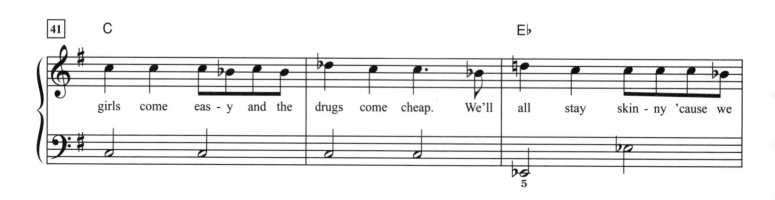

girls come eas - y and the drugs come cheap. We'll all stay skin - ny 'cause we

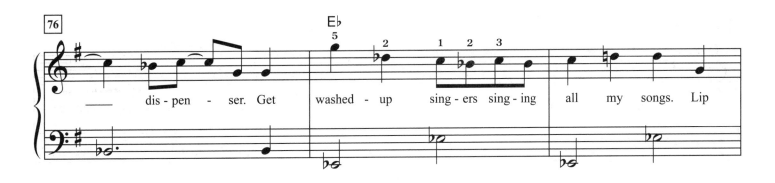

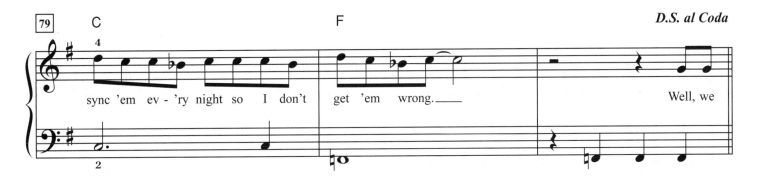

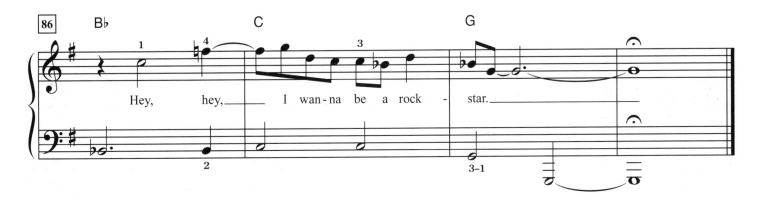

Verse 3:

I wanna be great like Elvis, without the tassels,

Hire eight bodyguards who love to beat up assholes.

Sign a couple autographs so I can eat my meals for free.

I'm gonna dress my ass with the latest fashion,

Get a front-door key to the Playboy mansion.

Gonna date a centerfold that loves to blow my money for me.

I'm gonna trade this life for fortune and fame,

I'd even cut my hair and change my name.

(To Chorus:)

Touch My Body

Words and Music by
Terius Nash, Christopher Stewart,
Mariah Carey and Crystal Johnson
Arranged by Jerry Ray

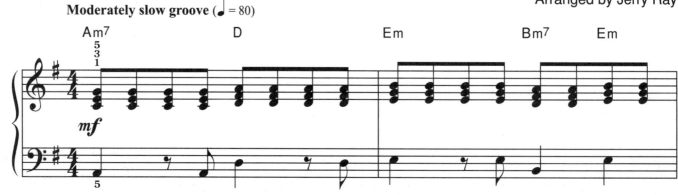

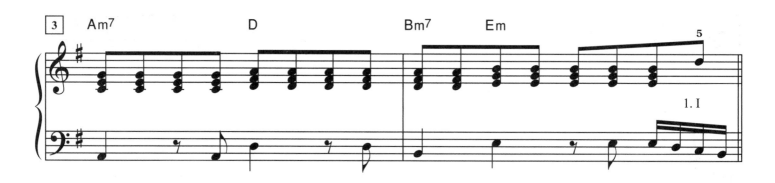

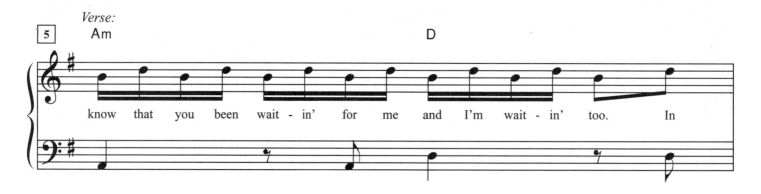

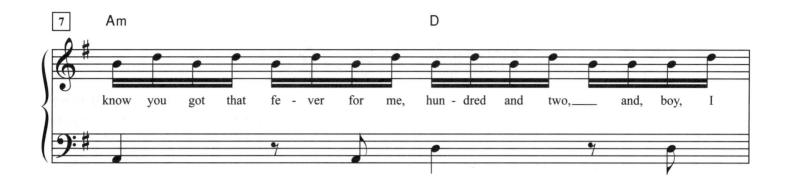

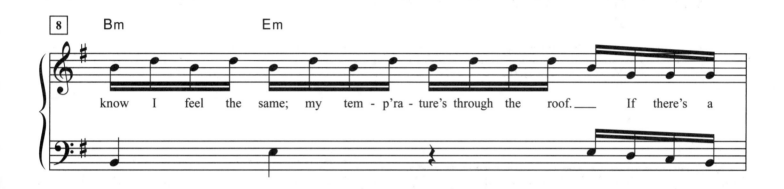

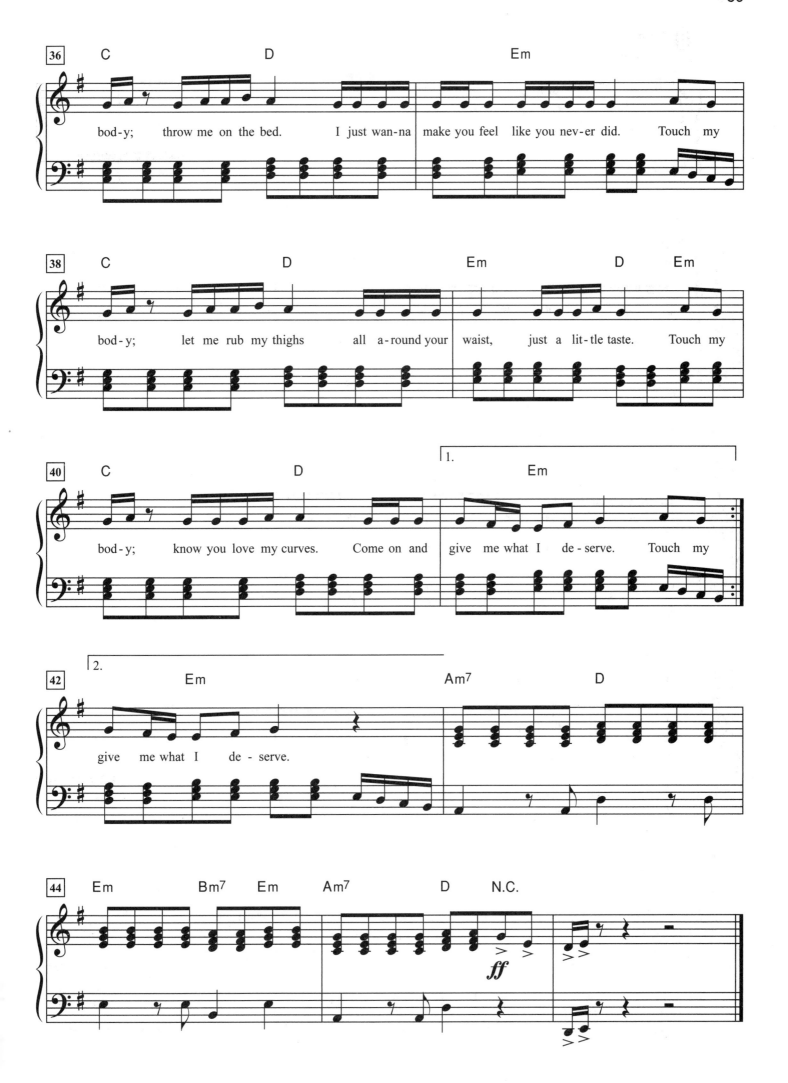

So Small

Words and Music by
Carrie Underwood, Hillary Lindsey and Luke Laird
Arranged by Jerry Ray

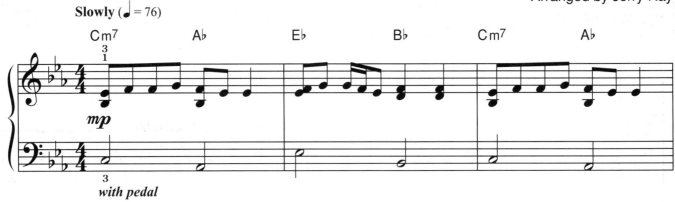

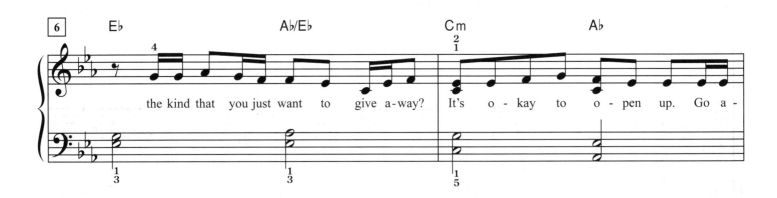

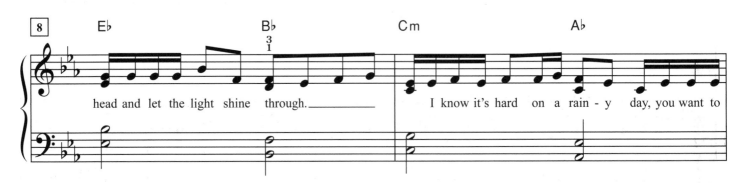

Chorus:

35 times that moun-tain you've been climb-in' ____ is just a grain of sand. __

38 And what you've been out there search-in' for for - ev - er is in your __

41 hands. Oh, and when you fig-ure out love __ is all that

44 mat - ters af - ter all, it sure makes ev - 'ry-thing else seem so small. __

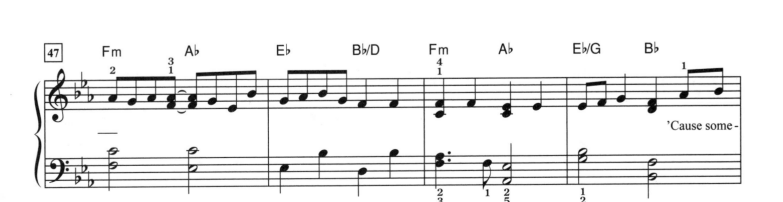

47 'Cause some -